theLAZARUSpoems

wesleyanpoetry

ALSO BY
kamau
brathwaite

the Lazarus poems

kamau
brathwaite

wesleyan university press
middletown, connecticut

Wesleyan University Press
Middletown CT 06459
www.wesleyan.edu/wespress
© 2017 Kamau Brathwaite
All rights reserved
Manufactured in the United States of America

National
Endowment
for the Arts
arts.gov

ART WORKS.

This project is supported in part by an award from the
National Endowment for the Arts.

"Lazarus and the Sea" by Peter Redgrove reprinted with permission
from publisher Jonathan Cape. CIRCA 1970: Photo of Alice Coltrane by
Michael Ochs Archives/Getty Images. "TamCC" and "Vicissitudes"
© Jason deCaires Taylor. All rights reserved, DACS/ARS 2017.

Library of Congress Cataloging-in-Publication Data
Names: Brathwaite, Kamau, 1930– author.
Title: The Lazarus poems / Kamau Brathwaite.
Description: Middletown, Connecticut: Wesleyan University Press, [2017] |
Series: Wesleyan poetry | Includes bibliographical references. |
Identifiers: LCCN 2017018700 (print) | LCCN 2017019567 (ebook) |
    ISBN 9780819576880 (ebook) | ISBN 9780819576873 (cloth : alk. paper)
Classification: LCC PR9230.9.B68 (ebook) | LCC PR9230.9.B68 A6 2017 (print) |
DDC 811/.54—dc23
LC record available at https://lccn.loc.gov/2017018700

5 4 3 2 1

Contents

Introduction

When one begins & undertakes(!) the ard-

uousness of dealing w/*carême*. shipwreck. the des-
truction of one's self/*entero* in all its circles cycles
& affections as a result of assassination. death by
Cultural Lynching as i have to call it. one begins to
uncounter ghosts of the imagination. basilisks.
chimera. winds blowing from the underworld & wo-
rd we kno not where. bleak & deformed ancestors.
torted self-images . the issure of spiritual blood
from the middlepassage — indeed the recognizing
that this osiris crisis imposed upon this body of the
soul here at the beginning of the 21st century is >
one more re-ply *(yes)* replay/response to the catastroph
(e) of slavery — the most — *need i say it?* — comprehensi
-ve & long-lasting traumatic event in (modern) hu-
man history. preceded by the Black Death/Hieronymus

Bosch and echoed later in Holocaust-Hiroshima-9/11 its
Abugrave Guantánamo and other conseQuences. . .

So as i journey into the otherworld of this Xperien-
ce/i say. i begin to meet the reveal(ed) Xcruciated
avatars of hope (& hopeless)/rebirth/return – Lear. Chr
-ist. Orpheus. Osiris. Alice. Dessalines. the Wilson
Harris time. the Tutuola figures of **the bush of** <
ghosts and above all LAZARUS – the only hu-
man being known to us to actually return alive <
from dust within the dead

But this return and its enactment in the word or i-
mage or movement of art . is crazy w/paradox/dis-
appointment/failure and contradiction as we learn
(yes) from Peter Redgrove's great Lazarus poem – the
only such poem known to me in the English language -
and i just had to celebrate his contribution in Pt 1 of my
own agony of seQuence

Nvr have i had so much fraught & obstacle & amb-
ush interference w/a poem – interference into actu-

al txt - doubt ragged edges sabotage of form & for-
(m)lessness. the failure &/or indecision/dissoluti-
on of intention/images. the dissolution/resolution
also having to walk thru his own wasteland recog-
nized between the two 'great' modern warres of Eu-
roAmerica And is Eliot who at one time identified
himself w/Lazarus come from the dead to tell you
all/tho he was not nvr *IN* the dead as is Peter Red-
grove in his poem (below) and me now in *mi carême*

At the heart of Death – alongside its ?opposite or con-
trast **Immortality/Eternity** – is the phoneme & phe
nomenon of the end of Nature – Light Space/Time-No
mmo and what we call *Consciousness* – Love/Feeling/Memory
/Vision/appetite/sexuality/horizon And 'Beyond' this is <
Resurrection – Redgrove's great theme – wherein one has

to be re**N**atured (Wordsworth i think wd have known this too –
see also Yeats) – behold again the wizard Light – be/come un. bli-
nd and recover Consciousness & Speech. be/come like 'ordin-
ary'(?) again - the miracle of absolute reTransubstantiation
and the agony of that

This that follows is only my Beginning. w/my own End i cannot imagine that i will endure the X treme lyric & miraculous integrity of Lazarus but my xperience of cultural lynching has allowed me to think in dreams about these things even w/out the holy words

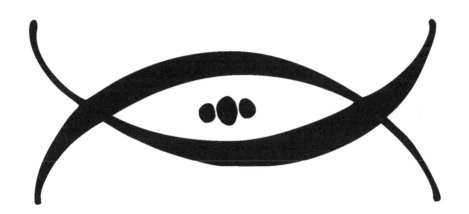

Peter Redgrove
Lazarus and the sea

The tide of my death came whispering like this
soiling my body with its tireless voice

I scented the antique moisture when they sharpened the air of my room
made the rough wood of my bed – most dear –
standing out like roots in my tall grave

They slopped in my mouth and entered my plaited blood
quietened my jolting breath with a soft argument
of such measured insistence – untied the great knot of my heart

They spread like whispered conversations through all the numbed rippling tissue
radiating like a tree for thirty years from the still centre of my salt ovum
But this calm dissolution came after my agreement to the necessity of it

Where before it was a storm over red fields
        pocked with the rain and the wheat huddled with wind
Then it was the drifting of smoke from a fire in the wood
        damp with sweat . fallen in the storm

I could say nothing of where I had been
But I knew the soil in my limbs and the rainwater in my mouth
knew the ground as a slow sea unstable like cloud
and tolerating no organization such as mine in its throat of my grave

The knotted roots would have entered my nostrils and held me by the armpits
woven a blanket for my cold body dead in the smell of wet earth
and raised me to the sky for the sun and the slow dance of the seasons

Many gods like me would be laid in the ground - dissolve –
only to be formed again in this pure night among the blessings of birds and the shifting
water

But where is the boatman with his gliding punt . the judgment and the flames?
These happenings were much spoken of in my childhood and the legends
And what judgment tore me to life . uprooted me back to my old problems and the family?
charged me with emptiness for this holy simplicity?

<Here is the kind of poem – power of image/voice/imagination – written about the same time as my 'At the death of a young poet's wife' - that i wish i cd write! The Cambridge magazine *Delta* i think (1951/52?) in which it appears – i don't yet have Redgrove's **Collected Poems (2012)** - is among some thousand items stolen from my NYU apartment 2004-2010 which witchery and **cultural lynching** (CL) engenders these what i call *post-CL poems.* but fortunately and wonderfully, i still have the recording (to music) done to several of these Cambridge poems by Zea Mexican & myself at Saltpond Ghana 1961/62 and this Redgrove, read by Zea to the piano of Chopin, has been transcribed by me here (CP 27/28 feb 2013) - the poem's format following ZM's breath-lines since, as i say, the Peter orij was not available to me in txt or on the internet. Finally find GOOGLE BOOKS 1 march 2013 w/significant diff format. But i retain the Zea. Peter (d/2003) was a fellowpoet friend of mine at Cambridge - both of us 1950-54 – <<
who pub some of my poems in *Delta*

The Poem

reBurial(1)

When that Person die, before separating from the Persona or Spirit, there
is first of all the NINE NIGHT WAKE where we all keep company - the community <<
of the living w/the community of the Departing Light and the unBorn Ancestors

the 21 Days KUMINA follows when the PERSON has been buried on the NINTH day
and begins a journey of unMemory into **kalunga,** where the Person and the Persona pa
rt company at the CARREFOUR - at the crossroads of Time

the Person then journeys for 40 days to the 'Space' of the Ancestors - the unDead
- while the Persona travels for the same period of time towards the world of the BO
-LOM/the unBorn

At the CROSSROADS of 40, the Person is reBuried and becomes open to a new futu-
re/possible Persona; while the 'first' Persona becomes BOLOM and begins the journ-
ey back towards the Living to find a new (as it were) Person. but none of these move-
mants & reincarnations can take place until there is eventual reunification of Person <
& Persona on the xtreme dark side of **kalunga.** This is possible because just as the <<
Persona is the 'shadow'/'spirit' - **TWIN & OPPOSITE** - of the Person; so does the
Persona have its own TWIN & OPPOSITE, one which returns at 40 days to the Cross
roads of Return; the other which journeys to the XTREME DARK to await the arriv-<
al of its reBurial before beginning its own journey back to (re)Birth - the reLiving Li-
ght

The reBurial allows the Person, w/*its* 'new' Persona, to be recognized as a Spirit AN-
CESTOR so that the reBurial is in a sense a reBirth but in the Spirit World where
CROSSROADS/CARREFOUR have become MIRROWS - mirrors of soft light you can
walk through in both directions and not only self/self but also self into OTHER & vi-
ce versa, since you are now dealing w/DOUBLE REFLEXION - reunification based on
a spirit principle similar to diurnal tidalectics, as referred above w/TWIN & OPPOS-
ITE

5

reBURIALS take place in familiar enVironments. where life is. As a seaside people, th
(e) p/of my community observed a seaside reBurial - the procedure of which is in the
twin & opposite mirror image of baptismal reBirth

The earth body is taken from its shallow protected grave (cf **Namsetoura**, who was nvr re-
BURIAL w/all the conseQuences for herself, CowPastor and the community of CowPasture and by xtens-
ion, since she being like a sole 'survivor' now speaks to & for Barbados, Barabados itself and even beyond
Barabados for the historical Plantation community of the Americas as a whole, tho there are no doubt sev-
eral other but still unrecognized unheard Namsetouras elsewhere) and entertained (welcomed back)
w/another NINE NIGHT - tho since this is for a *Personaless* Person returning from ‹
the Dark, this NINE NIGHT has to be observed when there is NO MOON and lasts
from 9pm to 3am of the period, w/drumming & instrumentation only on the last two ‹
Nights. The singing begins w/Midwives Nights 1 & 2; women of the household, relati-
ves and close friends (males inc) Nights 3,4,5; the entire community 6,7.8; and the LA
SS NIGHT children only - the closest we have on earth to the *bolom* unBorn

The colours allowed into this DARK NIGHT NINE NIGHT night - unlike the first NI-
NE NIGHT where people wear their ordinary workaday clothes the whole time and go
about their everyday business, observing no special diet or procedure – xcept that
the music (singing, drumming, testifying etc) is Cumfa, Kumina or Wake – and black/dark
for the first 3 Nights, blue for the crucial midPeriod (the belief being that the Spirit ‹‹
can only see Blue Light – and that therefore ALL MIRRORS shd remain covered w/the same bl
-ue cloth used to coVer all mirrors from the moment of Death to the arrival at the CARREFO -
hence too the BLUE cloth of water under the Pagoda of 'reBurial' and even deeper the GREEN
sign ofthe Living). On the last 3 NIGHTS and all during the reBurial, the colour = the
White of Celebration And while the first NINE NIGHTS is a feast, this second NI-
NE NIGHTS (from 1-dawn) in a FAST. (more & more) food & drink is allowed-in only ‹‹
during the final cycle, w/a great 'Carnival' at the conclusion of the ceremony

(When Harriette & the People go downstairs. they will prob begin this Carnival)

On the beach, with the sun coming up, the Body is committed to a moses, scu-

lled from the stern by a single fisherman, the boat decorated in the form of a yellow scallop or sea-shell, since it is Agoué whose domain this is on the shorewater. The family, friends, memembers of the community, well-wishers (and you can't stop the time < of the curious and today's tourists!) will accompany the Body in small boats (themselves fill ed w/Harvest/Offerings) to the (floating anchored) Platform or fishing-boat (the **Pagoda** of this DS) a short distance offshore and of course there will be a great singing and < acclaiming congratulation dressed in white on the shore

for the classic Haitian paradigm of this Occasion, see for xample Gérard Valsin's 'Céremonie Agoue' and used in my poem 'Agoue' in **Jah Music** (Savacou: Mona 1986), **Words need love too** (Nehesi: St Martin 2000;< Salt: Cambridge 2004); and *Waʃafiri* 42 (London) 1 July 04. Above all, see the remarkable correspondence of this 'reBurial' txt w/that in Maya Deren, **Divine Horsemen** (1953)

[In cases, however, when a Child dies and is to be reBuried, the Child's Mother stays on shore and does not accompany the boats across the water to the Pagoda - that CROSSING THE WA TER being a representation of the journey of the Spirit along the **kalunga** of the underworld << as well as the MiddlePassage - the two journeys being now enmesh(ed) in interrelated memory & ceremonial MIRROW]

the image of PAGODA appears in the poem because, for one, its an MR cultural ideogram (see KB5, **MR**, 2 vols (2002), pp141-144 & passim); but more specifically because what the assembly of small boats is moving towards is a three-tier ALTAR [see Geo E Simpson, **Religious cults of the Caribbean. . .**(1970), p170]. the reBurial rituals of course taking place - *tonnelle* - within the belly of the fishing boat or on the first (largest) flower of the floating platform - that area marked off w/woven palm-screens from the view of the general. . .

In the Pagoda, will be the village *ounghan* or priest or shepherd, assisted perhaps by a *mambo* (particularly if a woman or, as here, a child, is involve), *okra* [see n. on p7], *baba(s)* & *hounsi(s)* and of course Visiting rankin *serviteurs* from other communities even nation (s), might be present

The Body will be WASH(ED) as Harriette says in the poem, to (literally) reMove grave dirt, and to fortify - fructify – the flesh w/the clove & myrrh & frankincense' of em balm to prepare it for the final 40-days journey back to reunite w/the Persona and from there on to ANCESTOR and SPIRIT and even perhaps *Iwa* or back on the other (oja) side of the mirror to eventual 'reincarnation' thru the BOLOM (see wonderfully - Toni Morrison's **BELOVED**)

*African ceremonials are accompanied - cannot be w/out - the **OKRA** - the child who contains/carries the soul of the family/kin /nation/group. When, as here, a child is to be washed, the okra is esp important, since he/she becomes the spirit/mirrow of the trans progression. . .

reBurial(2)[1]

The Chile - she sai(d) - the Mother said –

Our Lady of the Crossroads
as i had call her to her husbann the Scarcecrow on the way
to the tabernacle of the Burial because i cdn't remember her name

- Harriette Herself -

when she was young when we was all young
before the illness that had brought on her death

. slowly withering all her haunts of underground & branches
. the sandals of her voice her smile the frangipani flower

and des. Troy her family leaving it in red carabs & wooden spli(m)ters
when she no longer here

but she is here today at the carrefour - quiet & beautiful & nectarine as ever - in a white closely-cut but not tight cotton short-sleeve muslin dress w/her calm arms of the pure bright bay. like Yarico. xpose - looking - sometimes leaning - out of the hi gh window onto the wide beach out to the sea w/its near-distance & tranquil dis-cipline & quiet blue colour where they have taken the body of The Chile **for re-<**

Burial. . .or as she xplain. . .

'for a washin'

---

[1] When i am growin up in Barbados (c1945), i come across, quite by accident, climbin over a wall at Gravesend, << near Needham's Point, part of the old (1780) British military Garrison (Fort Charles), this beautiful graveyard by the sea and i seem recall that someone wrote/had written a poem about it, 'Graves by the sea' (lost in the CL). is amazing how some 60 years later, in this DS, i have returned so unXpectedly to that Gravesend moment in this DS of 're-> Burial'

touchin him down into the cade water again. because he had become so stale >
in the last day(s) of the harVest. w/ his poor slim soul sep. aratin from the bread of
his body . the sweat from his marrow . thought from the shape of the face of his <<
family . no bloom . no bolom . no balm - as if he was wrapp in a painting. . .

and that is what they was doin out there. about 100 years juss beyonn the white
cast-net sur. face of the shore. in like a little **pagoda** of water. some kind of delic-
ate shed w/a darak slanting maroon roof of palm-leaves. and there was like a car
pet of bright green rec**tang**ular water around and under it - like some kind of wel
-come or ceremonial mat in the midst of all that quiet blue *winti* and there was li-
ke many more little boats - battoes & moses & pirogues some lookin like small tugs and
tubes and cigars also out there on the face of time. but little more than matchbox-
es in size from this distance upstares lookin down. and it was like they wasn't movin
they was so slowly movin out there towards the pagoda. and at first you cdn't ev-
en tell if they was moor. ing over the brown beach or the shallow mar & which >>>
was beach & which was the water from the eye of the window. since it is all the >
same colour of Quiet & mirrow & the smoothenesse of a slow slow processional
pic. ture & groove. until at last they reach the lime of the white surf and the water
growing in that deep indigo blue of the future

So that when you look(ed) from that high upstairs window of praise w/so many <<
peoples crowd. ing w/their lean curv(e). ing silent necks & faces lookin all-togeth-
er thru that high window of space as if they was bunches of flowers & branches of
harvest nodd. in in the slow wind and the wide open eyes in their heads outer-look
in the ocean like so many black seeing pomm(e)granate tamarind seeds

and so many people also seating. crowd. ing the corridor as if they
was still on the ship co(m)in over from the ancestors and so much el-
se also goin on - so many coming@going along a long stream of si-
lence of hubbub - tho the main reason&eventure was what was ha-
ppenin out there on the bright salt that had drawn so many of us out
&up into that pale seaside building of community. coming from so <
many different whispering doors&directions in their many layers and
cyars & on foot towards the wood and the gate among the trees <<
whe the cemetery was. all these years. and the manchioneel beach
i suppose right behind it on the seaside look. in on and how the small
boats - the little battoes & moses & pirogues from all this distance lookin down. . .

goin out to the pagoda of the Chile w/all these st lucia mangoes &<
oranges. the crown(ed) heads of golden dominíca pines . and in <
one of the moses boats up front. the gleam of the warm ribbed re-
compense of nutmeg. and you cd see like the yellow dots of the gra
(pe)fruit & viridian streams of like sugarcane & the pale musical horn
(s) of what must have been a god or goat lookin out from one the <
batteaus. and another moses bleedin w/river-cherries. and sometim-
es the glitt & glitt/er/some/times not/from what look like bungles&<<
footfalls of straw. and a govi of water and two long thin bottles of <
chili or kumquat infuse w/vinegar for Agoue the surly watery lord of <
these reaches . as was our custom on these beaches. . .

and i recaw that i hadnt been home to my own sewing & sea (m)stress
rockin-chair Mother for quite in the while and my sisters were like angry
& angular waitin for me an refuse to help me w/what it was i was suppose
to be tryin to finish. some homework of drawing or poem of water or canvas
of history . title-deed of unmemory and eel

So i give the place like a walk & stay out all night under the bright <
needlework & the feast of all these stars so soffly feeding their dead/
still thinkin of Home and the unfinish canvass of hungar & spectacle.
and at four-day i had join the forthcoming unity of DunLow & BayLann <
on the way to the tabernacle of the beach to witness the reBurial marass fe Harri-
ette Chile . and i look. as i say. down the depth of the window but cyaan under-
stann what was happenin they in the shallows - all those delicate miniature boats
and like slowly moving sea. horses from so high up lookin down and they was like <

movin slow. ly now back. wards towards the shore as if my clock **STAP** an i
miss sommnn an i cdn't tell *whe* the Chile was among all those distant slow-movin
jewels & shaegoes & somebody tell me - and it wd have been Quiet obvious once yu
know - that he was in this like likkle yellow double-scallop and yu cd see it move.
in up & down up/down . more or less in the miggle of the pic. ture that somebody
was painting and like the top part of the lid of the scallop was a little larger than
the bottom lip as it were and it was move. in up. wards & awaay ver. illy gently
from the lower - as i suppose the tide tugg. in at it made it from time-to-time do -
tho it was clearly no doubt still hinge at the back to the other part of it. self - as

12

scallops of course are and they was still all these other small boats of armour arou-
nd it - *etchin in light* - like itching for the future eyes of the sunlight – most of them
shine/ing w/memory in an attendance of stillness . all comin back <<
now w/out fruit from the fisherman jetty & shrine and the water had
been like stripe into four or five strips of time - like on the page yu juss
leave. as ifa was a **di^ination** or *warri* . but runn. in from like beach
to boat or rather now from page of pagoda to our beach of beads
and not side . ways from Amurica to Af. rica as i have to write it from
leff to right across in this poem . and from time to time in between th
(e) stripes where the water was clear . yu cd see like down to the ver
illy claro of it where there was like these little *blim-blim* stalks of quiver
in green gracilaria lookin like the long thin leaves of spin(e)ackle w/<
speckles of red on their brochure . or stringing streams of pale living
sprays. dark slender sings of dark-blue waiverin stilks hardly movin >>
lookin like the shackle shanks of familiars float. ing down into the wa-
ter of sounn w/out the sound of the pain that ferry us here. w/out >>
any sound at all really

at these cross ⁿroads of anchor

these hundreds & hundreds of likkle black glittering bodies so careful
ly arrange w/unangular anger & lying out on their backs in a long cl-
ose row together on the page of water i still tryin to write . their long
thin needle legs of *lucumi* drift/ing off/drift/ing on into seaweed of >
echoless history . and below them on the very verge & verdure of th
(e) ocean . the shade & shadow of a bright refracting cannibal an-
gel. dress(ed) in the long flowing red angles of an old and infamous
political party. ijs arms spread out like the wide watery voice of the >
middlepassage. along the distant flatbed of memory

but i didn't stay long at the window because as i-say. so much else was goin on in that corridor of ifé and two of my rival girlfrenns was < sitttin there opposite one another w/mwe standin in the miggle of th (e) life between them tho only one knew who the other was - or so it seem(ed) to mwe in the mirror - or rather *discerned* what the other was/who the other was - because that other was talkin all the time . one foot of her jeans-pants cock-up in comfort & confidence on the indrani chair or satellite settee or solfa tho she seem(ed) at the time to be reeding from some thin threads of musical paper or *quippu*-li-ke spinnin silk-cotton sea-wheels of whisps thru the air and Nemesia was watchin her watchin her altho she too appeared to be reed-ing from some fading folding silver spirit-level of ifá that she was takin from the rose of her warm furnace bosom and no doubt plottin to kill Herenítza who was really quite innocent but i hope strong & content & able to bear w/her any sudden treacherous assault from a jealous

And the young people were also sho(w)ing me their sea. sonal draw ings of insistence. some w/the same kind of bodies i had seen float-ing like seaweed under the page & pagoda and St Elmo my young-est uncle alive come w/a very talen(t)ed young lady just beginning her dreams whose work was or had been in the teeming xhibition << somewhere in the bui(l)ding and it was a v/beautiful refleXion w/its own vivid& astonishing poem of the dangerous indigenous cannibal angel i have seen in the water already. stitch now inta her canVass of mirror or tv. which she recited quick. ly & xcitedly for me in her ow-(n) quiet ringtones. as if from the spool of the sea

but when i get back to the window of words all my sense of the sh-ape of the time had been change and the reBurial procession had disappear from the sortilege . all the boats w/their quiet wakes of de corum out behind them had gone as if they had nvr been bourne >

14

and there was noth. ing out there on the beach of xistence. no ma-
(n)go or yellow or golden or gleam or recompence or dolour of nut-
meg or grapefruit or muse. ical horn of what might have been god
or goat lookin out from no longer batteaus and eVen the sea and th
(e) timeless pagoda of return had gone from the mirrow and i had
the impression that Harriette and the morning and most of the crow-
(d)ed people in the corregidor were getting ready to go down to
meet the heartshape of the cortège wherever it was in the mirror .
but the sea. as i say was now absent & hardship and all that was left
out there on the wide breath of the beach were these long stains of
distance where the cyars or cigars of reBurial had dragg(ed) like
snails or sea-roaches' soft chains across or just under the now surf.
less sand and there was only a few pieces of white fluff & paper
blowing about. cli(n)ging & si. lently tumbellin across the weed of
the wind like dry widow bundles of sargassum or strow and it was all
so silence &empty &sad &ungalloping bleach w/out harvest or harm
-attan or harbour. as it now is in the teenager picTure. because i had
miss(ed) it - not seeing the Chile come back to the Shore . And i de-
termine there & then from my sep. arate soul that instead of goin >>
back home to face the lonely heartbreak hotel of my Mother who
loss mwe. i wd sleep over w/Herenítza Accoumfô the Beautiful & sea
what might marassa again in the morning

Baptism Poem

The singing Sankey Gospel congregation carries you forward
into Hope
your hot flesh naked under the sinkle cloth of the cool water
soft flowing gateway to another life

As you go under you will remember the trees & the houses
along the shoreline where you lived among the thistles
and the smooth boulders of the river-bank and the memory of red & green
under the water where begins a different singing

and different drumming dove & fish & Holy Spirit
In this swift sweep of the new world now this middlepassage
of yr virtue now there are these hands & ribbons dressing you
. these new fonts of faith you do not understand .

I felt a presence on that land, Kamau. It had a patient, serene, windswept quality to it. As if
it was waiting for something. I saw the pond, or what is left it, the lone bearded fig-tree. It
did feel magical. Was it my imagination . . . ? – (And) *if it was my imagination* – all the
better. For that is what we will need to do – imagine worlds that defy the. . . nightmare that
presently holds the world hostage

You come back to the spluttering air the silver water in yr hair
and running down along yr face this smile upon yr heart
this new & certainty of step as you return to shore

19

What difference is there in you now What Shepherd of strange change
enfolded by yr loved ones . smiles & tears & revel-
ations. a blossom scent we share each other petal
one by one together
how to become & earn new light new life from strangle

<23 june 2013 . 6:25am>

[the francais font insert p15 is from nourbeSe philip's unpub 'Meditations at CowPasture' Sept 2006]

1/Lazarus pleads w/the poet fe help im out of im wound

You have asked me to come sit talk about myself w/in the image of our 'heritage' and yet you have refused/declined/have been unable to recogni ze nor not been told/how i am dead. killed by the Basilisk w/out psalm or

funeral advice. abandoned on the hillside. my ashes blown & blinded in th (e) wind. w/out memory or video >< Are you afraid of something? offend- ing the Dark Force perhaps? the ole Colonial Colonel? *Let them tek what*

dem want to take – leave me alone! How can i speak/participate in 'project (s)' w/out surface or soldier or solstice (?) w/out the consolation of justice or justification – for all that i have lost. been plundered out of plenitude &

usefulness So many bees these days on dead leaves w/out a glimmer or the hum of honey. is this how you want it go? tit for no tat? the hammer hitting not the brass tack but the writing fringer? Only you. my cousins of the spir

it. can lock my eyes out of the silence. bring words back to my tongue coat ed w/the rough & fiery skin of the lizard. Only you w/hopefully yr under- standing. can bring me back from the dead wall & valley of the thorns

But you refuse to me this gift this glorious benefice of yr slow winding coral voices. no blessing comes out of yr souls/yr mouths retaining closed even as i remain lock. down inside this journey on the hot devil's limestone rocks

2

There's such an emptiness on this hillside in this hollow wind of oblong bo-
ne-sockets of my eyes that can only hear you/hear you/hear so little much
in this dark sepulchre w/out premises or saviour. Lamentations cannot he-
lp me here. My old smile is wrapped-up in the cerements of myrrh and their

woven overlapping graveclothes cannot heal the minth

i can hear the coming of the Lenten season and the priests w/penitential <
sibilance & beads. the green trees wilt & weather in unbearing and attend-
ance even tho the days are long & true & beautiful like sailboats sailing on
the blue

i wish i cd remember where the sky is

sing the sand song of the shak-shaks/but my eyes are sad and narrow and
are no longer sparrows. no longer less beholden. at night there is the swee
(t) sweet smell of travelling harvest from the hiss and agone crackle of the
sugarcanes on fire/but the taste upon my wasted lips no longer liquird limn

or kaiso

the chirp/less in my ears no longer cuatro

3

Less Beholden

Less Beholden – in my dreams
Less Beholden – among these trees
Less Beholden – upon the face of this cliff watching over these waters

Less Beholden – the glint of blue and the hint of gold in the streaming
Less Beholden – these great passages of travel over the time of ocean
Less Beholden – the blacksmith the carpenter the man who shoes

        the horses - birth of my mother . the chapels
        of the living graveyards and the inhabitations of the dead
        the gift of wood in the place i build -
        the grann-duck rocking past the pleasure of the pasture w/her long golden
        line of ducklings. the sun in all its brilliant mastery of the east
        out of the distance of wonder. the moon riding down
        to the close of its eye on the last clear day of the year

Less Beholden – my memory of you and you walking w/me over the stone-
        fences . light of the stars and the flight of the sparrows
        and the shining obdurate blackbirds of the Revelation

Less Beholden – these prayers . my fingers playing an alight marimba
        in the shadows of yr black & nefertari hair. yr face in the wind of its mirror
        looking up thru the curved glass of the rainbow

        the rain walking over the roadside's green verges. the dark
        metal swinging in its steep portical of space over the countryside
      the bell pouring its petals of sound over the high cliffs and the precipices

Less Beholden —

Less Beholden —

      my song w/in you singing w/me here at the ending of the world
      where less is so much more . so so much more

      Beholden —

<16/17/20 april 2012 . "Less Beholden, [East Coast/Chalky Mt area] Barbados, is a place located in Saint Andrew region at 13°13'0" north of the equator and 59°32'59" west of the Prime Meridian" . rev 27 feb 2013>

4

O Lazarus my lover

O Lazarus my lover the first begotten of the dead
eat this salt bread of flesh from me
let me say Amen and Armagiddeon unto the sinners of the sabbaoath

for i have no voice now out of the land of giddeon
no more brass bleeding spokes from out yr broken Strident
this crisis of my feet over the river Jordan   .   walkin upon the waters

<6 march 2012 . 1:50am>

5

How Beverley? How you?
i don't xpect an answer/the ball-point pens have lost
the many ink their tubes of writing
and no longer produce trails or trials songs
from the glinted distance of the wings of birds
no coo in the cool of their woo-
doves . the sun-
substantiation of the legendary grails are not now note w/in yr

substance of

-planitation . nor any falsetto question of the Word

6

He rise up during the dark time of salt
in the blue solar sky under the famish hammer of the harmattan
. is at this time that he remembers surrender

and the unfurling flags of the middlepassage
how the cast cats of the dark
howl to make love after midnight and lark-light silver scratches on his ankles

like after the cutting of cane
and the dry dusty distance telling of bells after rain-
fall the colour of cutlass & worm

He can toll you nothing anymore
now he has lost all the cherish teeth of his youth and his mercury
And it is well past the peace of his midnight

7

Beech tree fallen among dreams

'. . .leave the stump of his roots in the earth, even with a band of iron and brass, in the tender grass of the field; and let it be wet with the dew of heaven. . .and let seven times pass over him.' [*The Book of Daniel* 4: 15, 16]

Outside my window in the cold
w/in its nether artificial necklace of grey bricks
an old beech tree upon the side-

walk blighted - perhaps by streetlights opposite -
so that it cannot sleep or seed w/in the infra-red -
perhaps of lightning -

so that it cannot see the dead. their dreams .
its blinded roots no longer find their way to watercourses -
perhaps its age -

here since perhaps Minetta stream - the hang-
man's corner. the death-door dungeon banishment for slaves -
perhaps disease or heart-rot banging like i feel - who knows -

its leam leaves growing all the seasons seasonally green until is time
to fall and falling all the years i live here - twenty now -
among the whirl of daylight wind & pigeon flow

amidst the nightly planets & the storms & police sireems -
        is cut down - down-fallen - in mid-October Fall. the brown leaves
        going gold. white inland seabirds clustering in shafts of flight -

leaving a great new sabre light & space
        at this round westem end of Washington sQuare Park
        among the younger beeches . new place . new Park . like so much more new light

Here on the pavement lies its stump its grave its epitaph
        all in one terrible neglecting jumble moment of activity and silent unforgivefullness
        Those who come now - walk here - stumble a foot. step on the former trunk -

wd nvr know that it once stood - w/tall & spread-out branches leaves
        and sparkle shade & night-time dark & star-light shadow. some-
        times sorrow - and how it miss the Quick birds now

        and how the Quick birds miss her where she was - their rectory w/in the Park
        its special colour sensé place & contour in the neighbour-
        hood's uptruding buildings tarmac tamarack & wood & water flow-
        ing through the flat & silver marshes to the river

But here it is this morning - disc of the fallen sun itself
its wooden wound - the amber colour of its curl disgrace
become its face - dim when it's overcast & bright & golden
when the itself sun comes out - like now this windy morning

by the winding road - ancestral memories -
its rough gnarl jagged bowl cut by the saw & ruin(ed) by those teeth - no
vaunted circles on its plain circumference - no
overt sign of pain upon its cosmograph -

but quiet smoky grey stryrations - agony
no doubt - but nvr doubt about its build of bulk
the seismograph of wind & storms that blow here thru her history
when she was growing up . her shadow on the ground .

tho there's no sense of gender as we understand it. growing up .
its stump stepped on by passersby who - as i say - will nvr know
its history of tale & poetry - will nvr hear its ancient song –

while she lies here - squats here - stands now alone in all her absence here -
                    - mother of her leaves' migrations -
aligning herself each daylight better to the sun and to the open sky

                    and growing slowly back towards the next millennium
And all this time - in the cold falling wild - the sQuirrels tirelessly stop & thread
    and stop & thread & thread again their golden tales among the living trees

They cut the beech down dawn one cold snow morning 5 jan 09
leaving the sun-face poem that watch-back at us all time long
& 'remove' the stump in the late winter darkness of that year

in early Spring 09
they 'erase' the stump & mark the sidewalk absence in a badly patch-up clay-coloured irregularly constructed sidewalk scar & unpave(d) grave

when the rain falls. amidst the mess & dirty settle sidewalk water. w/in the ugly cement sQuare
if you look closely. there is a clear round bole-shape pool where you see sky branches birds flying briefly by and parts of people walkin –
their heads their feet their careful silent torsos – all in their various ways invoiding the absence of the tree as they once did its presence
and in both instances . acknowledging

<9 ap 09 . 6:00am>

8
The Sideways Cauchemar

It's not sudden death –
heart - brain - miscarriage or even worse –
unimaginable really - and impossible to contain –
the death & burial of yr first-born child –
It's not like flood or hurricane or drought or famine w/its thromes –
too too much rain or none at all –
that you can give statistics to – nor Quantifly the suffering -
It's not the sudden loss of sight or weight or star –
the footsteps slippering on the stair –
the trip-up in the last curve of the famous race –
the apple dangling in tears beyond the finish line –

It's not like anything to name or share or even fear or care for. no
little totem animal or tidy teddy bear
It is a state of nero being. unbeing being. w\out the trace of faces
a dumb humming down beyond surprise w\out no
sunrise after all among the glittering seagrapes at the bottom of the grave
. the end of it and yet no end of it. no shelf. no less & less.   no
narrow cowrie shells. our unique plural selves w\in these
jumbie sentiments.   yr eyes in space far out w\out their sockets.   no
love\light anywhere.   even inside yr life's most precious sonnets

<23 jan 2013 . 3:30am . rev 28 feb 2013 + 1 march>

scenArio

Guests

To arrive at CP at 6:15am when the <
sun is rising silver out of the sea behi-
nd the poinciana tree. the sky soft im-
agination azuli. the dawn's pinks and <
yellow orange just disappearing and <
the whole early morning body bathe
in the slightly chilly breeze of a bajan
dawn of this time of year w/out flow-
ers just after the hurricane season

The Guests. w/in the sound of birds. will assemble on our freshly-cut front lawn. seated. for this Occasion. in the usual musical charade of chairs painted pale choral or gardenia (not the manufr-acture white). In this way (the way they are seated) they will see and feel upon thei(r) faces. the full glory of the sun's hoi-st after sunrise where it begins to sh-oot hot silver into the sky from behin(d) the shak-shaks and the tambrins an(d) lays down a shimmering carpet – al-so silver - on the now far-off and for-gotten waters out by Chancery Lane < and Paragon

All the trees on the pastor which our
guests face on our morning will be >>
in dark green silhouette and the grass.
as i say. freshly cut. will be its bright-
est shining green like newly born sh-
ade w/here & there a darker eye and
out-cropping of coral

The family and the few closest friends
will be standing on the porch. There
will be no greetings and no speaking
of voices among the seated genders

Colours of
wear

Children will be asked to wear white.
Young women will wear pale yellow
buff or cerasee w/emphasis on youth
& future figure. The mature women

& the mothers will wear sparkle deep
viridian or turQuesa and the old ladie-
(s) will dress in their silk of traditional
black or egyptian indigo. Hats will be
optional for the older women. but <<
preferred. The younger females and th
(e) children shd be bare-headed so we <
can see & admire the locks & braids &
the cornrow stylings of their holy hair

Men will be in the usual black suit an
(d) tie or in national or 'ethnic' attire

Choir	at 6:50 a small choir will approach a-long our path to CP. rendering a mix-ture of hymns and Kamau's favourite songs. If Gabby is present. he will sing his anthem 'Emmerton'
The Execution	Just after 7 at the moment when the >> sun's position in the sky turns the vegeta tion black. w/bright now gettin hot now steel-like ray-themes from behind the dar (k) and some large birds like frigates fly crying out from tree to tree. creaking al-most like parakeets and some woo-dove (s) cooing like from the Bagvadhgita and dogs barking in the distance. Kamau will come out from inside the house . dress in

one of his well-known tams and a dashiki
and he will join his family and the few cl-
ose friends of the porch for a moment
and will be speaking very Quiet w/the
soft dark wife of his generation who will
be bare-headed her head shaved her chee-
(k)bones painted *adinkra* white & adored
in a sea-blue *asooka* like Ada Yemânjaa
wear. Then he will come down the red
porch-steps. walking slowly among some
of the rows of guests towards the poinci-
ana twined w/a frangipani. under which
there will be a simple cedar box or flat-
form. He will kneel down there a short
while while evvabody lissens to what mu-
ses the morning now provides – the Quit
(s) the whippourills the dayclean/rainbirds
in the bougainvillea And then as he place
(s) a knee on the box and bows his head a

....   sli(g)htly forward like Gary Sobers being dubb upon his shoulder shoulder by Her Majesty the Queen. a mas(k)ed & hired > Xecutioner will come round the seaward side of the house and swing the blue sky up from the ground and cut off the head > of his languages

10

You don't have no memory on yr consonants where the black grains are
the rain drifting off beyond the future of horizon
the pain lock(ed) into the armour of yr heart
vainglorious like the flags of the defeated left shredded on the battlefields of the belovèds

All these stories that you used to tell the chilldren
listening in the mango season to the murmurous moonlight during the years of spiders
It is such a long time nowadays.   no salt in the dry cities
and the dead spirits llying among the leaves of the grasshoppers

A late but valentine poem

red seeds sparrow dust so many feathers in the universe
i kiss you once and it was far away and for a long time living here beside you
loving the orchids growing out of yr heart
gathering the roses & the amethysts

12

i am the man of dust this hillside of all fortunes
turn to dis-
trust the sun no longer burn-
ing in my head
or forehead w/its waves .   tone-

lessness is how i hear the whistle of the wind's wing fragments
of a bird's bones' nest-
ing in the grass inside the rustle
i am like Lazarus going to the grave
and i can tell you all and all i know of what i know of nothing

<26 feb 2013 . 10:47am . 29 march 2013 . 10:55pm>

47

13

Miracle
Mary Morgan Brathwaite

In 2093 my sister Mary is diagnose w/cancer. The first thing that happen is that all the doctors at the UWI (Mona) Hospital and a Bajan op-theatre nurse < there – since they all kno & loved her – declined any fees/x-<< penses and so did the UWI Hospital generally so that in the e-

nd, she get a *refund* of $Ja+<<
2000 - *'those were the ainchienne <
days'!*

But the miracle is in the dream
she have soon after the chemo-
therapy begin – when you someti
mes, it is said, begin delusions >>>
dreams & visions. transmogrificati-
ons. openings or enclosures of the
spirit –

There is this pounding she cd >>
feel and hear and SEE – four ho
rsemen through the window ga-
lloping over & across her chest
– the noise the thundering - and
then they were gone out throug
(h) another wisdom

. . .

And then this single horseman
which she kno at once was Chr-
ist and that she *heal*

. . .

This is the story that my sister tell me during my carême, had write it down, she say – can't find it now – but had first share it w/a small gadderin the Dorcas leag -ue her Church in Jan94 altho w/hardly any - [strangely] – a res- ponse from them she notice or recoil

. . .

How easily we ignore each one anothers' needs reject each others' miracles and manacles

But at the time, in the hospital – or rather at home now where this wa(s) happening - soon after the Visitation, that same night, her Spiritual Advisor the Rev Evans Bailey come to see her to who she say the story i juss tellin you << and his first Quetzal & Concerm was. what were the colours of <

the horse/men and was there a<
pale horse and she remember th
at voice had said in the vision <
'There is no pale horse. . .pale
horse'. . . which in the *Book of
Revelation* = Death

And so there was no 'Horse. .
. Pale Horse'. . . and so the Rev
said *That's Good* . you're going
to live . And so she did

Amem

14

for Lazarus. . .i fear. . .the miracle was nvr perfect. . .see Peter
Redgrove. . .see those peoples in our townes and villages citie
(s) and our universities some of the doctors in our hospitals. .
. who walk Quickly very often. some more slowly. their arms
fix always at their sides. their feet along carrying them alone.
They are alive the oblong shape of the grave always w/in the-
(m). They look around only by turning their holy bodies roun-
(d). their watery eyes always unfocus beyond you/no matter >
how wittily skilfull you may be. how idiot. their noises in the
air. it seem they cannot smile. Something of the other word
remains w/in their preference performances. If they are ma
rried they are unseldom seem about their spouses. ditto their
friends. if they have any of it

it cd only have been a blemish just before twilight
but already the ibis had lowered her head in slowest regret
in the pond-grass. and it's too far away now to be undone
to bring the light back . and the sound . and the good wishes

how can you de-resonate an echo
and the unseeing gong-gong where it come about?
bring the gold back into yr irises' recesses
and the shadows of the water?

love will have to return into this cool pool also

w/salt speech ocean distance w/out which there wd nvr be such nearness
. it is this miracle – or some of it – that will open yr eyes
up to their becoming . the blue sky the cirrus flowing
over the continent . the sources of the rivers and the ancestors and the stars

but it is too much this great passion of creation
no matter how much you had wish it
only Isis had been able to do it . even tho my flesh was in fragments
. now there's not even the raindrops of its moments

. not even sibilence

16

the 40 days where i lay dying

mystic in my heart . illumination running through my veins the whips
the pain slanting towards the sunset & the sleepless rain-
fall . i hear yr voice in the whispers of eleggua at the corners of the parishes

wind warning from so far away . in the valleys . windmills . nothing
reaching me from heaven . his emblem these smooth black kukoo sticks
. i cannot come to you tomorrow where there is so much sorrow

<1 march 2013 . 3:15am>

first Light – birth - the Beginning – once lost – cut
out – heart's broken retina
- can not now nvr be regained/repaired/un
-knotted from the passion of its lattice bosom - veins & memoria & blood
- the Orpheus cycles and those mysty islands of forever trying to reach home

O Dessalines. even tho you will become our first own Emperor. you can not
nvr now reopen yr eyes up from the issure of the dark spiritual wound of Africa
pouring into the passport of the middlepassage. unable to surprise
yrself from the fragments of yr unXpected death & vision

18
Life is not song or resurrection
gong-gong

the Black Bess/Less Beholden goddess in the red dress by the river
the rice fields' *bissi-bissi* . the mandingo's weather's where & wither
in the balafon

And so i hold you hope & softly in my arms
and we both weep from harm

19

There's so much contradiction in the weight

of resurrection as we learn from Redgrove's poem
from Lear too and Alice and Kawamuinyo's lyric
so much undone to be undone. Creation's uncreated dread

to then put back together. Nature unable to speak
in simple syllables like the poet Dobru did
What is the opposite of **I AM** beyond time and yr mother?
and where is yr mother now among the crowded dead?

<6 march 2013 . 12:10am>

20

Ghost of the Morning

This morning i get up about 10 after a late late night
of many of these poems and the bedroom door ajar –
when Bev gets up earlier than me these days
she'll close the bedroom door so that perhaps i sleep
w/out her noise of up-&-down & cleaning up the palace

As i wake up this time i feel i hear her in the sitting room outside
and when i go out to say Good Morning i see her standing there
and so intent on looking/reeding at a sheet of paper in her hand
she didn't even see or hear or notice me so i surprise/move clos-
er since i curious to understand what cd be reeding so intently in
the silence but the more i move towards her the more & more sh-
(e) move away like shift. ing from me w/out moving like towards
the front door which when i reach there is no body there and th-
(e) door still lock from lass night's lock&key and there's no way
she cd have moved in front of me towards the workroom or the >

kitchen but still i want to check and call out *Bev*/and she was far out in the backyard w/the pumpkin green & bonaviste & plantin black-eye peas & guinea-corn So was this something in the eye-lash of the moment like a dulcimer? And yet i still cannot believe that anything inside my eye of sound cd have created this clear shape and so familiar person reeding on the paper going back & back away from me receeding nvr moving as i come out towards her disappear in this bright sun. light meaning of the morning

<2 march 2013 . 11:55am>

21

Alice in Wonderland

for Rutli

White Rabbit in my work-a-day black sleep
you look to time to lure me out

to peep and ponder out the wonder-
land that lighted up the garden of your heart

How i had longed to know how time
and lonely arts had lighted up the garden of your heart

And so i fell. when following up the thought

But while my heart was upside-down in air
(not-knowing child. not time-

suspecting then) i see you disappear
through key-lock garden doors

and find my heart still pounding after yours
shut out by unexpected locks of hum-
drum time

How i had longed to round around the work-
a-day to find the lighted wonder of your heart

But changeling sleep and wonder-
land White Rabbits will not
last.   and when i wake

i find no time to follow up the key-
hole clue that speaks between our hearts

And you have thrown away the golden key and left time heart-
less in the now no-wonder dark-
ness of your heart

Alice Coltrane

22
VOYAGER (1)

TONIGHT OUT ON THE VOICE OF THE PORCH
IT WAS AS IF I WAS STANDIN ON THE BRIDGE
OF A SHIP OF THE PASTURE W/THE WIND

BLOWING IN THE DARK AND ME ONCE AGAIN
CROSSING THE FUTURE OCEAN THROUGH THE SWEET
SMELL OF SALT AND THE STARS' NEW SILVERY TORCHES

NOW THE RAIN HAS COME BRIEFLY *(11:40pm)* AND GONE
BACK *(11:44pm)* INTO ITS CLOSED VOICE AGAIN *<11 march 2013>*

23
VOYAGER (2)

I WANT TO FIND A WORD OF MY OWN FE THANK ‹
YOU ALL THE BEST BEST WISHES HOW I LOVE AN
(D) CHERISH YOU HOW I WISH YOU WILL NOT GO
AWAY THAT THERE WON'T BE ANY SEPARATING ››
RAIN. THAT WE'LL BE TOGETHER FOR AS LONG ‹
AS WE CAN HAVE ME THAT I'LL BRING A SMILE
TO THE CLIFF OF YR HEART WHEN YOU THINK OF
ME WHEN YOU SPEAK OF ME W/THE SPIRITS WH-
EN YOU REMEMBER ME IN THE GREEN QUIET HAR
BOURS OF YR THOUGHTS THAT THERE WILL BE ‹
NO MORE THUNDER IN THE DOORS YOU OPEN &
CLOSE IN ANGER OR IN THE COOL OF ANOTHER
WORLD THAT THERE WILL BE TRUST ALWAYS UN-
DER OUR FOOTSTEPS AND THAT THE DAYS WE LI
VE HEREIN TOGETHER ME HERE YOU NEAR AND
NVR NEARLY . A WORD FOR GOLD & ROSARY &
EVVALASTINGNESS . SILENCE & FIRE . A WORD
TO END THIS LETTER WITH AT THE BEGINNING ‹‹
OF MY LABOUR . ONE WORD FOR IT ALL. FORVA.
LIKE "HALLELLUJAH" BUT OF A SINGLE SYLLAB ›
 LE. LIKE TIME-AMETHYST OR BLUE OR KUMINA

fe DreamChad

24

i am who i am not
looking through these portholes of my distant protocols
passing from somewhere else to somewhere else
you greet my hunched haunt losses in the windward shadow
of my other self

i acknowledge my name when you call it – *yes*
and speak you through the window of some thought
some nother port of call
but it's not me sitting in this chair or sailing on this ship
i have no key left to open you the door

i am destroyed and do not want you see me in my ghost

25

If you cd have brought me back from the dead soil . punt or gondola or barge
even tho i've nvr kissed you in this blue earth's aureola
in the burning sunshine in the wildfires by the seaside . on the road leading up-
ward to the caves. past the long-ponds & the windmill widows and the bright accents

falling from the leaves. the morning after the sweet night of the jasmine gardens
of Aburi by the Pra by the Volta beside my dream of the Ganges
yr bosom of red spices . *kumbh mela* . cinnamon . *obosom* . the calm-
ing coconut oil of *santeria*

i kno you wd have said the word . made gesture of yr promises
called out to the sun to turn time back to balm
packed the black stars stacked away into their match-
less boxes. stood near me on the pasture and listened to the accent of the burning cane

and i wd have opened my eyes in the approaching silence
and smiled for all our histories to see
i wd have come forth as it was intended & foretold . as it is written in the holy books
and muttered under the slanting thatch-roof eaves of Bandiagara raindrops

i wd have taken yr hand even as you dissolved into the mystery of the unopened door
i wd have sipped you once more from the storm . the broken tea cup .
i wd have run out of myself towards the spirits and then back again into my own two feet .
smiling and listening w/out future to our little thrilldren

<5 march 2013 . 11:50pm>

26

Mandinka Yamore
Salif Keita & Cesaria Evora Ev#325E30

VI

27

THE SLAVE SHIP BELOVED

a love story

Dallas Mountains - Midnight 1 Dec 09
i move towards her . sleeping . in the dark . caress her thigh -
and she says. 'Doodoo. i don't know whe you are -
. . . from which room you touchin me from. . .'

$\mathcal{D}$ear -

i have leave the cycle of ancient reminiscence - John & Liz & Shivaun & SMaddy & the cleft garrulous retired red-face Colonel and im ~~likkle~~ dimpsey wife & many of the older Jamaican novelists who have out. live the war. and Geo Lammin (g) sitting to one side and other ladies & gentlemen whose faces i can't remember and a few select elder members of the east in that flicker- in circle of canebottom mahogany plantation desire – and have walk back. wards into the many rooms of this Old House. if it still stands and is not now dust beyond rubble. ₽ast the << room where we held our rehearshall ~~that~~ that night. ₽ast the two further rooms where i lay my bed w/the soft white cambric & embroideried San Juan Puerto Rican sheets and the matchless light-blue bedspread on which i see ~~yr~~ yr little African doll. shipp(ed) & fast a-sleep where yu have leave her/leave w/her so surreptitiously unguised towards the end of that dark door of evening & rende§vous *o Akwaaba Akosua of whispers* as you had lea-ve me to go back to her that night. tellin me lies that you was tired. so tired. that i shd go on back to the hotel w/the company. that you wd remain - stay here and write awhile and then lock up the place an come look-me-up later. at the hotel *not to worry*. how you so loved me as i loved you *O how i love(d) you*. and so i smile(d) and kissed you on the lips. lingering there for that moment in the sigh of

the rigging. press. ing amethyst against you and give you my own sweet tongue to taste
the salt of that long crossing the mint that tip of animal leaf of red brown sugar in yr mouth
for the last lovely time of the month. as it turn(ed) out. and went to the coach and climb-
(ed) up the ~~stubble~~ stumble plank an get-in w/the others and watch(ed) you. lookin bac-
(k) at you out thru the dark wash(ed) now moving views. sittin in yr cyar. pretendin to be
fiddlin w/the keys like some kind of banjo or harp or kalimba or thumb. piano of space . li
ke tryin to starat th engine that wdn't start or star. light re. flecting from the noc. turnal >>
sunlight that you are . as if you was goin to follow us after all an lookin worried about it un
til we was out of sight of the land

And i have gone beyond that room and beyond that room again twice to what must have
been the last room at the very end of the shape of the ship and the time of that House or
almost the end of that Time . the soft little fragile silver flick. erin torchlight of vespers in
my hand . and this brown wooden box . cedar or cypress. still ~~smelling~~ smiling of myrrh.
and this ~~letter~~ ~~litter~~ letter. if it survives. if ~~it~~ they was not found by the Capuletts. And i
was lookin for somewhere safe to leave them. *these precieuses*. whe they might not be <<<
found . whe they might be overlook(ed) in the narrative . in this dark narrow passageway

of approach. if i was lucky. **W**hen i see this little latch just under the window-seat. to the
neetha side of it. in the deep dark future of the wall. like a faint little brooch of decora-
tion or spider of deception . and the catch open to my touch of life and there was this litt-
le recess. **a real likkle koumbla** . which the builders must have ~~re~~ reject. ed into the sto
ne. and so i place(d) the box into its side as if it might heal these slow wounds of palim-
drone. and on top of the box . this letter . which. as i say. if i am lucky. you will one day <
find . if you arrive . —a— . if you are still alive in this desert of denial & falaise . the room so
empty of moor . ~~o my be~~

In the box are our photographs. several of them. a selection ~~xxx~~ form me of the dear

-est guests of our memories. images of you & our happiness together. The letter tells

that i am ^pregnant w/you and i am going to be the ~~mother~~ murder ~~metaphor~~ of yr child

Yours . yr belovèd

28

Défilée

for Joan Dayan & Djene Small

About noon on Friday October 17, 1806, not three years after he was declared
Head of State & Emperor, Jean Jacques Dessalines, the Liberator of Haiti, successor
of Toussaint Louverture, was assassinated by soldiers from the South on the road
from Marchand two miles to Port-au-Prince, the capital. His shot & stabb-up body
was stoned & torn to pieces by his murderers & left, it is said, to be found & taken
for burial by the 'madwoman' Défilée, a meat seller *(vivandière)*
reputedly the Emperor's lover once upon a time

Bright thrones have been cast down
before the leaders stripped & torn from power. fled or dead
Dessalines my liberator my xecutioner mon Empereur

my lover of Pont-Rouge like this
who break the bread w/bloody hands who tear
the nation flag from Blancechette & make it red

& make it blue. unfurl it new. where now it stands
for slave & bloody cloth & resurrected
bone. who throw the whiteman down

from his plantation towerhome at Cormiers at Vivières
the crackle axe of musketeers
against La Crête

Now here w/out yr head w/out yr virile hands. bereft
of Claire Hereuse. of balls. bereft of eyes. yr ears cut off from music. matross.
cannon. chasseurs. racheteers

tendresse of love pulled down into this mud
where no clouds move
across the sky where no stars stare their stone

where no wind blues where no sun shines
upon yr skin. where the red blood un
-gurgled from yr throat now flows & flowers flowers

O Dessalines so so cut up
O splendid coat so splendidly cut down

Cows on this cow pastor all my strife provide me meat . goats. blackbelly sheep
are here. hens. turkeycocks jack rabbits rare but sweet. swift bones
so full of life

each morning to yr door i bring this little covered heap of victuals. the long dark
face i so adore. the fingers on the plate the morsel to your lips my love my pain . plain
sacrifice of my sweet flesh upon yr palate yr plasaj . O salvage

warrior you how chop me up
you chop me down into the howling hot prostrations of yr love
O how i love each shaken silken golden moment of yr power

Now into this coarse pig-stain macoute i carry w/me everywhere for years
it watch my rape. witness

my papà and me-màmà-mè assassinè . how Rochambeau come keel-
down all me bredda-dem and my two only suns

inside the Cahos mountains. trick Toussaint off
to Franche till i go mad w/all this blood
this trekking death down in this mud

betrayals . maroon dark nights
mornings of rendezvous
quick anxious crossing of the river coming back to you

mules on the edges of high trails of mountain passes
my mind cooing w/the mourn of woodoves all day long
watching myself like blackbirds at my door

criss-crossing imperfections chiring in myself made mad
w/manananse working working working
above the star-bed strawbed ceiling of my floor

Now sit i down beside you in yr pool of blood
w/seven wailer demons in my head po
fool. to let them fling you down like this from yr I

horse. yr vision of a people marching on. out of this dungeon hearse of slavery
into some proper light
no blight no more upon this crop of koromantees on this broeken shore

An so dem cut yu down before the morning crow
befo the crowd dat might have save you
gathered on the road from Marèchand two miles to Port-au-Prince

the meat they make of you i cannot sell
tho i sell sutler meat at Ogoum all my life
the fragments of yr body's dream i can but touch

O cruel piece by piece i can but gather from the entrail entrance of the blade

There's no peace here
gaps/gashes like a hot milk boiling over
and the furnace burning our tomorrows spoil our race

Duclos my love i cannot find yr face
this is your head wuhloss my love my love
how tenderly i love these harsh Dahomey
scars. adinkra whipmarks on yr back. the prison bars

you break with these once hands from which you flame
Is this one eye i find wrapped in the grass of years?
i cannot find the tongue you kiss me with & spit me wit
and when you spurn me. turn me out. i sit down at yr door

and wait for morning take me on to Fort St-Clair
or bring me back into the bed & spur & warm of you
This lip torn from yr skull i find near clammacherry bushes here. its strip of skin
still living so it seem

to sneer where it shd smile. Mile after mile i walk
w/you mile after mile i walk for you mile after mile
i fight i hurt i heal O ride Arada ride. this is your angel
bone this is yr broken hand. the ruby ring

still blinking on yr flinger O this can this can nvr nvr be
how they dis. member how dis. honour dis-
remember you. assoun my bell my open door my fate

                              and so i pick you back each plwé & pluck
                                        & root & memory & flower
                              the toes back to the fit of instep & the ball
                                        -bearing ankle weight

and let the one
foot if it be one
foot walk quickly down the road

let the slip hips dance. fit fairly into place around the ready loins
let us make love again & laugh the belly there the guts
the navel string the strange high knife of noom

. assemble me yr lungs again so you may breathe
like wings and shout commands. turn the horse round
and gallop off to victory à Bois-Caiman and moon

let me ride with you général. let me ride with you
in these dark eyes i will restore
in this fine head i plant here in this place of burial

O Dessalines O Dessalines Lazare Gangan
O magic makandal
& sun & flag & plaçage . nanchión

chimera

you has to dead first . lose it all
every precious pouring trombone moment
in yr valley . every night forever w/out light or rest or mango of surprise

every last sweet tongue drained out its very speech
to find the way back
home if you have not yet entered heaven or its hell

you will first have to find yr skull and listen to its mental bell
ring deep inside yr empty bone
yr head shaping itself in yr new mother's moan

to wake naked again in the dead womb w/out eyes or night
endure again the pain and skill destroyed you
the long journey w/out bend or silver in the water

and the pebbles you find here
the thin bridge fashioned out of hospitable footsteps' shells
and the soft stones across its river shapening yr spine

but you can't create this conversation till you can walk
w/word. even tho you still w/out the limp
of speech. even tho you reach now into the terror of the mock
-ing whirlwind underworld

Here begins the shape of yr palms and yr fingers
wrapped into the curved gesture of yr faith
. this will open yr eyes though there is still the labour of darkness and rock

. this will open yr mouth
even though you can't yet suckle-up
the wine of the sunlight and the roses

but yr father's fire has been entering the future of yr mother
shimmering & crackling over her flowering pastures
and the river is now flowing into its estuary. the mangrove
and the marshes. the first wild fish and the guave

obdurate lobsters. yr flesh at last healing from reptile & pain
. the time you have now found wavering into green shadows
like casuarina filigree of fire. even though you still not able
to stand upright inside the burial

. so much undone to be undone . fashion(ed) and again un
-done to be undone. so so much distance flow
before you find the harvours. and so near now the shallows
O so much light Osiris . opening the time of the sand & the sunlight

& the flowers

<16 march 2013 . 5:15PM w/three basilisk interruptions but the poem still ends 17 march 2013 . 1:27am/now 3pm w/love>

old woman at the  crossroad . the blind

eyes bandaged blue so she can see me in her skin . no words
sign me my death is not tomorrow
there is no hour called of old or new
her language lingars into me inside . like chilldren muss be seen not heard

She is the mambo konnu of Eleggua
who brings her dry crossed guava sticks to heal with
i hear this tolling wind so many oleander years gone now
my ears receive their massages as if i was a saint or martyr of the desert of the morning

She nvr smiles nor gives me time of day
this place is not for greeting
i cut my hollow out. She sees it too
Her eyes are wide awake behind the blindage of my sorrow

the stick she offers will not break the wreckage w/its wire
Say nothing she advises to my listening . no thanks no condemnation
She tells me i can only go so forward to go back
you now too limp and lame to make the evening newes
But keep the faith she mutters to my faltering as i pass on to go not why or where

There is no music in this valley dry as rain and feeling
. dark sun she sees in flood w/in the three salt loaves of desolation
Walk Holy . as i pass she whispers in my imagination . Walk Good
Nothing more blessing than the distant thunder

<13 july 2013 . 2:55am>

195/120

Here where the dark clock steps out of itself towards the midnight
the crickets cease their cherryping
the silence shuts off suddenly after its lingering delay
the sea freezing all along the howling coast. its white border-
line goes out . the moon no longer rising

. i know i have been where i have not been .

. the living and the dead .
the old worlds that we use for these disusèd things
these moments w/out space . the ambulance w/my dead body in it
stalled in traffic. outside the watching windows of my house of glass

O devastated Gaza

time lying in its bed w/out a movement
somebody writing syntax in to memory before my time
where there's no word or wind or hieroglyphic

i did not know that i wd drain away w/out this pain & passion
is plain to see there is no rain or nevermore
my navel-string unravelling from underneath the banyan in the backyard to the stars
Nothing is soft here anymore . silver no longer hard w/glistening
no light beneath the lime tree as the ancient poets say their lyric pictures are

It is too easy to Xplain and yet i cannot tell you Help me
This is a wasteless frontier w/out monument
w/all the vanQuished spirits standing in their places
w/all the constellations w/out voice or picong
whê people do not hear they own self lissennin they song

32

And now i hear the voices from beyond the grave
the urgent whispers of my sisters wishing me come back come back
this even when i cd not find my feet where my sleep was

To know . even so long before . that this was going to happen
a miracle like breaking bread & fishes & walking on the water & the wine
Something that really doesn't happen tho is happening in you

That the dark dirt they packed so tight around you
stone fall on wood and cracking on the casket
wd become flesh again & bone . rain
falling on the traces of yr blood . strange deportations of this stranger of arrival

When it begins it will now nvr end
The opposite of where you had become
The night you cd not see the light transformed to stars w/out their wages
how you stare blankly up . so many immemorial millennia
what we call silence going on for what we call forever tho it was only like a few days like ago

That you wd have to breathe yrself back into the bright spirit of the mirror
so that you see the horror of yrself when you can open yr eyes out
and lose these twin and rival bleak vertiginous enclosures
these dark encroaching hedges of your vision

How to remove the desperate flowers from yr throat
the rats from out yr solar plexus and yr bowels and yr vermal eQuinox
let the green fields grow yr skin back in
before yr face reaches the blossoms and the haphazard thorns their season

How you will remember every parable of twilight & folk-garden wisdom
each cussword every splendour of the unforgiven
let yr tongue back towards yr appetite and speech
and find a way for yr old heart to be already grieven
. Time lying in this dream w/out a reason .

The weaknesses that lay you down so low . so hollow hollow hollow
import the grey & bluish muddy glauze w/in yr eyes
the mourning morning turning from the nine-night forest howling hurricane

it is as if they snatch the amankrado's golden chain from round my neck
my poems have no jewels or chameleon left
i hardly write my own regard to reed
my imprecisions blurred . forsaken . beyond their murmur syllable & meaning

there is no sound of cymbal in my Nommo
lips can't sing song . words cannot flaw along the floating river
the verses flat. no bit between their teeth. no poem breathing w/the wind along its mane
no flame or loveliness of memory to name

And yet i gather from the pasture how the birds sing their frail nests
on to new . a few precious picot pieces of stripped cloth . somebody's combed & shredded paper
a length of string to weave with . two crossed sticks shaped like the ascent of light to heaven
and the curled kite sleeping w/out wings into the cloudless graveyard of the blue

Lazarus foretelling *The tortured Christ* / Guido Rocha (Brazil 1975)

carrefour

s a long night and will go on like forever – they have so many proto-cols to recognize so ma -ny factions & coalition (s) to appease that we will go on waiting out here in this Garden to well after midnight. When Govvament don't want sleep it don't. The Judas Guards will probably not arrive in the pommegranate air until > well after 3 am. just as the cocks begin < annunciation of the cusp of dawn. We << ourselves have been out here in the chill air since 11 o' clock soon after the Lass < Supper and the strange washing of each others' feet . i know it's been a long day and a funny night – you tired & scared & more human than ever so you want to sleep even if you think you don't want float away into the deep blue cascades & corridors of the distant sea but cd yu not have stayed w/me at least one hour? Is not easy being alone and eaten by these termites' crises all by yrself. A little helps a long way on the way: a word even a grunt xchange acknowledgment will

do to kno somebody else's eyes are open under shutters . that there's a wat -ch & share. to sweat blood all alone inside this dark int easy. cd you not stayed w/me like one more hollow hour? The sleepless bed the sweating waiting – room the operating/xecution chamber > whe yu are dead or bourne again/It is as if the tall pine trees have broken down w/some dry sycamore and have been spl -it right down the long red body-centre of my heart. The resin leaking from them is my blood. like on the wet brown paper package in the butcher market. Like you /i will be three days in the cavern here > and when you call i will begin the journey back/untrap the cerements from around my feet & fetters so i can stand/unwrap some from around the **palo pîèl** > of my belly till i can feel my thin hip/bone (s) jutt out & hurt as they begin to move against the wooden cedar casement and then my hands are free unwrap the dry > clot round my face so i can see the gree (n) out-side and move in. to the dread & eldritch light where i am still unwash my <

hair in tangle rastafari thorn my breath a
blast of plaQue and rotting teeth. my >>
smile when i can smile is yellow like the pill
-ow pallor colour of my death/There sh-
(d) be thunder down the lumber of th-
ese eucalyptus trees but the shorn bark
is too torn and silent for me to lean on/
hear. There is no Ogoun in the mirror of
the twilight here. for Xango blaze this pla
-ce is too far dark & damp away for his-
trionic miracle/This poem writes itself w/
no/or little faith The nim tree cannot >>>

crack me open nor the olives sing into my
soul. My head is only half/way here and
there(')s no proper light to see w/i still >
breathe injustice and it makes me sneeze.
i seem to be half/human as i walk. i hear
birds wing pig's squealing on appeal and
the bright sparrow sorrow song along th
(e) hill/But there's no room for gold or
glory here. i am the casualty of a miracle
not the amazing grace of terror that trie
(d) to make me whole/again. This is **no**
country for old men. i am the stammer >
not the stradivario/i have no howl or ham
-mer to break thru these locked locks to
speak this jugular

95

34

i've come to the stage where my [now] words are like dead
    bleached-out crabs upon the beach w/out baptism
    they cannot move or weave me comfort or eQuation
    i cannot even speak them from their shells of flies

    We move to Death from old age . end of yr lime
        here by the sea w/its soft tides
    the constant move & murmur of its wise wide immortality

        But Death from Disease
    and the induction into this by yr culturally committed murderers
    it is the cruellest infliction that you cyant adjust or find xcuses for
the lonely is Xtreme . the pain something no painter can describe or horror

    It provides no comfort corner and there's nothing anyone can say
        but tell the truth. find its right words or fail to recognize them
        find love in any of the oblong stretches of the line
        w/out a breeze or what used to be a proverb or a smile

    Even the crab's empty shell has left me for another safer haven
        even the flies don't know now how to bother mwe

pale travaille hollow & familiar schelle. its hole of howl
upon the beach almost under my crushed foot
. to pick up . dischard . throw further a way bleak . out

leave

where it is . time whispering its sand & glass & leaning water
or toss back to the walking sea
where it zigzags back down slowly to its dream & scalpel bed

. not learning any thing .

So many ruined like this chapel of such fragile loss
So so much silence where there used to be such samphire
So everything so scene . so similar

lazarus lass poem

Bentley Callender (July 1993)
Glenroy Straughan (Ap 2013)

No nuse no more the washing of yr hands
in familial supplication/prayer
since i no longer rise

still sleeping in my skeletone
into this strange ostrich light
like entering a gentle room where sun is setting

my skin dry leaf and weed. all sounds eroded. the woo-
doves finish. perhaps a little hostage rain.   pale
footsteps w/out print or echo. my green dream

losing its vein of colour in the ache
the lass grass tossing my dry bones down to shale
that stings me all along the pathway of my bleed

where i will move on thru w/out you anymore
o no amore
so little water in the song . thirst beyond tears . cool vinegar

where now i cannot sing the pond
where every drop has failed me drip by drip
words shaped by hollow omens. ear an urn

a useless desert all this poem
to not hear bird or voices' playful laughter
behind the line of bushes on the hill preparing for the night

no more communicate their flight or teasing moment
this cavern standing in the shadow of my monument
the cruel termites eating sorrow out the life you dreamed

like when at last i lie w/in the grave
the dust all round me in my mouth & lungs . soft eye-
ball bones. pants-pocket pouches cut-out so i can't throw stones

no longer able to arise the morning
unable to return as you as all of us has plann(ed) beyond this architrave

We is the loved one all the spirit now w/out the life you schemed for it . unable to attend you at this breaklight conch-shell morning . without a bread or fish or miracle or wall

37

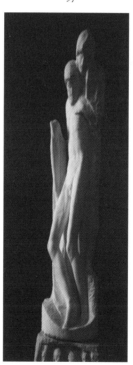

<adapt
Michelangelo Rondanini *Pietà* (1564)>

38

farewell Poem

for Cecily Spencer-Cross . this poem's first reeder . and Janice Whittle and the visual artists of Barbados
who created the occasion

i say farewell before i see you now
ghost at the door and spirit at yr window
the shadow on the walkway looking at you thru the louvres

. the bird-song you once hear . sing . ing in the ears of lovers .
i cd not write these lines if so it wasn't so
if there was turning back the years from this

i say farewell before i see you once again
in case i do not in these fields & hills beyond recall
that i have lived & loved like you w/you upon this rock

And even as i weep . as i must weep .
the clouds are bright . as they must be . above the eastern shore
where hidden springs pour from the limestone rock
and pastures know their billy-goats . and cocks who crow like clocks

And on the western shore . i lie upon the beach of youth or lay-float
until noon and kick myself upright when too near manchineels
. the rare blue moon

rides clear into the middle of the day and drags the quiet noisy water curling all along
the reef in blue & green & silver . and hope that grey gleam turret church
pun top de hill don't topple down before i turn to splash back home

Such memories the breakers bring me w/their soul
such vivid thirst of colour in the coral pool
and shak-shaks turn the blue atlantic into gold

and burn & drift it inland w/their sound
These bright tumultuous congregations always make us smile
the moko-jumbie casuarines between our house & heaven

All these i thanks & praise you raisin mwe . the kukoo-foo that sweetens out
our arms to rich & black & brown & warm & sensual . the okro in its magic casket capsule
up. holding us from harm .   the yam that keeps us steady and our eyes of bright

All this has made us what we are. we give back what we get .
the pailings' privacy . the mathematical aesthetic planks & genius of our chattel houses
that shd be made professors. construction conservation. waste not want
not . as yr life is . so yr memorial gourds . you live inside yr light w/out fan. fare

Now life is gone before i make it myself true
before the time i plan to sit-down talk w/you and lissen
like how you walk the country roads and look down on the glissen over Oistins Bay
and understann what Namsetoura say

Know how the Mighty Gabby play the igbo eddoe words of Emmerton
among his chords of islands and how you sit in-here this evening
wondering how can there be such soft so such persistent absence
such sudden silence in what juss yesterday was canticle & tambourine & incantation

And so i say farewell before i see you now
loved ones will grieve that i am gone away from shape & time & motion
like touch-yu-touch-me-back in duncks tree's love's intense emotion

And may mwe. as i wander. find pond & pool i have been searching for
since Lakes & Little Bay . not stand here in the dark
and lost before the vast stark endless ocean
and nvr find my land . and lose my friend

VII

Revelation

<found improvise poem in the peaceful environment of MR/MR (2002) just before the Cultural Lynching>

Closing yr eyes
opening up all yr senses
memory . history . into all this darkness
of where you come from
light/light years circles spirals stars
galaXy of the Great Spider Ananse Melquiades

whatever is all . whole . old & new-
ly born & what we hope home will be eternal
metals that do not tarnish . bones
out of continents of coral . polyp steps
into more than Pyramids
beyond the soft phosphorescences of whales

yr faith in this coumfort . these trees
you plant that will not vanish
sustaining you & all the Ancestors
all these rough generations. the seed (s)
of unceritain future

reach. ing it out to give it shape to give it touch
that you can hold to give it grain to give it voice
in the presence of these grave Nommonom

First lightning then thunder
then the sound of the sea
making itself from its mirror . creating

the rims of the world . all the islands
& the continents . & as far as i can see
all that i can travellingly imagine

w/these oracle
the door opening for. ever into Mother
the flower's resurrection from the tomb

all this perpetually golden world
how we depend upon the sun's up. rising
even when there has been pain

even the moon . even the spiders
sleeping . even in the rain

always the branches of noon in their vast forest
of fortune . always the mystery for-
ever of the dead & the whispered children

who bring them curled here
from which star. from like which brief earliest leaf
i nvr really know

i am i/am i/am i/am

The anXiety in all this makes me stammer
you cannot say how it does not matter
me . you . neighbour or desolation

for i believe in what i have . this etch
of knowledge of becoming
the Light . it seems now. of all ages

the stretching edges of the ocean
in the diurnal deafness of its origen
even in the desert where the salamander inches forward

w/the colour of its miracle
without which there is nothing
. bird . plant . owl . wave . anima (l)

Corruption failure & xtinguishment
will be the opposite of who i am
the opposite of what you know me to be not

.

closing my eyes in the darkness
to open this grave of the world

Jason deCaires Taylor . detail from Grenada Grace Reef drowned slaves underwater sculpture Project (2006)

40

The sea is now white sound after the whale
has finish washing the valley quiet as a bell

Jason deCaires Taylor . detail from Grenada Grace Reef drowned slaves underwater sculpture . 'Circle of Blue'/Vicissitudes (2006)

VIII

Opitennin

The morning that i stir within the narrow compost of my grave
miraculously ash space move around my head to open out my eye
the eyelids sticking down some time until they opening

That i cd lift my head and shoulders' shadows
find arms & legs to shift the crisp & sound-
less wind-like gravel for more company. push myself forward up

sit there w/in the dark of worms & soft-stones for a while
my nose allowing me to breathe the sticky myrrh of frankincense and bones
. and somehow light here too . and space . more space .

to push my fingers' hands up thru the coral up. ward up. ward
until i break into the peace and ancient sunlight of my birth
my one eye seeing all

the green the grass the distant tattoos on the trunks of trees
and then the trees themselves . their leaves and silvery design of branches
w/the wind within them swaying welcome

i cd not not believe it as i pushed up upright
see the blackbirds hear the twits a gaulin wing above me
like a kite and chilly mooring in the forgotten sky

its open blue as if my heart wd pierce it!

And so i push myself full up and climb myself out of the grave onto CowPasture
when something turn my head around and there beyond the chain-link garden fence
was DreamChad's washing on the line as if she nvr stop her washing after i had gone

And as i moved towards our home
the wind come up and blow the colours of the clothes towards me evermore

<CowPastor Barbados . March-August 2013 . November 2016 . Feb 2017>

abouttheauthor

Kamau Brathwaite, born in Barbados in 1930, is an internationally celebrated poet, performer, and cultural theorist. Cofounder of the Caribbean Artists Movement, he was educated at Pembroke College, Cambridge, and has a PhD from the University of Sussex in the U.K. He has served on the board of directors of UNESCO's History of Mankind project since 1979, and as cultural advisor to the government of Barbados from 1975–1979 and since 1990.

   Awards he has received include the Neustadt International Prize for Literature, the Bussa Award, three Casa de las Américas Premios, and the 2006 Musgrave Gold Medal from the Institute of Jamaica. He has received Guggenheim and Fulbright Fellowships, among many others. His book *The Zea Mexican Diary* (1993) was the *Village Voice* Book of the Year. Some of his many lit/culture studies include *The Development of Creole Society in Jamaica, 1770–1820* (1971, 2005), *Contradictory Omens* (1974), *History of the Voice* (1984), and *Magical Realism* (2002), 2 vols. Over the years, he has worked in the Ministry of Education in Ghana and taught at the University of the West Indies (1962–1991), Southern Illinois University, the University of Nairobi, Boston University, and Holy Cross College, was a visiting fellow at Harvard and Yale, and a professor of comparative literature at New York University from 1991–2011.

   Wesleyan published *Elegguas* in 2010 and *Born to Slow Horses* in 2005, which won the International Griffin Poetry Prize (Canada) in 2006.